WARNING!

THIS IS A CARLTON BOOK

Text, design and illustration:
© Carlton Books Limited 2013.

Published in 2013 by Carlton Books Limited.
An imprint of the Carlton Publishing Group,
20 Mortimer Street, London, W1T 3JW.

A catalogue record for this book is available from
the British Library.

ISBN: 978-1-78312-079-6
Printed in Dongguan, China.

CARLTON
KiDS

The publishers would like to thank the following sources for
their kind permission to reproduce the pictures in this book.

Key. T: Top, B: bottom, L: Left, R: Right, C: Centre

Alamy: /Leonello Calvetti: 26-27, /Rod McLean: 28-29
American Museum of Natural History: 23tr
© Carlton Books Ltd: 3, 5, 6-7, 8-9, 10-11, 12-13, 14bl, 14-15, 16-17,
18-19, 20-21, 21t, 22-23, 24-25, 30-31b, /Vlad Constantinov: 23br, 29
Corbis: /Klaus Lang/ All Canada Photos: 26-27, Connor Stefanison/All
Canada Photos: 6-7, 12-13, 16-17, (background), /Torben Bellmer:
14-15 (background), /Jonathan Blair: 19r, /DK: 30bl, /Sandy Felsenthal:
20, / Louie Psihoyos: 26bl, /Kevin Schafer: 23bl,
DK Images: 27r
FLPA: /Pete Oxford/Minden Pictures: 13b
Getty Images: 11r, 12t
iStockphoto.co.uk: 10-11 (background), 30-31 (background), 31r
National History Museum: 7, 15r, 17
Thinkstockphotos.co.uk: 4-5, 22-23 (background), 30c

Every effort has been made to acknowledge correctly and contact
the source and/or copyright holder of each picture and Carlton Books
Limited apologises for any unintentional errors or omissions, which
will be corrected in future editions of this book.

DINOSAURS RULE!

The dinosaurs were an amazing and varied group of land reptiles. They roamed our planet between 230 and 65 million years ago.

Brachiosaurus is a good example of how later dinosaurs adapted to their environment. With sturdy feet to support its massive body and long front legs, *Brachiosaurus* could lift its body and long neck to feed on leaves that were beyond the reach of smaller herbivores.

REIGN OF THE REPTILES

At the start of the Triassic Period, about 250 million years ago (mya), there were two main groups of land animals: synapsids (including early mammals) and archosaurs. The synapsids were the most widespread and successful, but by the end of the Triassic the archosaurs had taken over. These reptiles were the ancestors of the dinosaurs and pterosaurs.

Earth was changing as the Triassic ended: land masses were moving and mountains and new oceans were being formed. The dinosaurs adapted to change and went on to dominate the world during the Jurassic Period. While dinosaurs ruled the land, large marine reptiles known as plesiosaurs lived in the seas and huge pterosaurs soared through the skies.

DINOSAUR DISCOVERIES

Fossils are the preserved remains of animals and plants. Palaeontologists, the scientists who study dinosaurs and prehistoric life, have built up a picture of how dinosaurs lived by examining fossils. Fossil bones give clues to their size and shape, while teeth and claws help us to work out what they ate.

BRACHIOSAURUS
(Brack-ee-oh-SORE-us)

LIVED: 150–140 million years ago (mya)
PERIOD: Late Jurassic
LOCALITY: USA
LENGTH: 23m

HEIGHT: 13m
WEIGHT: up to 35 tonnes
DIET: herbivore (plant-eater)

SCALY SKINS

Although fossils of dinosaur skin have been found, we cannot be certain what colours these amazing creatures were. However, by looking at modern reptiles we can guess that dinosaurs would have been patterned and coloured, either for camouflage or for display.

The fossilized skin of Polacanthus, one of the armoured dinosaurs.

DINO SUCCESS

Dinosaurs appeared during the late Triassic, about 230 million years ago and went on to rule the Earth for 160 million years. They were more energy efficient than their competitors. Having their legs underneath their bodies gave them an upright posture designed for speed and agility. Some scientists also believe that, unlike other reptiles, dinosaurs were warm-blooded and had bigger and more efficient brains.

THE TIME OF DINOSAURS

MESOZOIC ERA: 250–65 Million Years Ago

65 mya

CRETACEOUS PERIOD
The first flowering plants grew and conifers flourished. Cycads and ginkgos became less common. Dinosaurs remained the dominant land animals until the end of the Cretaceous Period. Small mammals then became widespread.

135 mya

JURASSIC PERIOD
Cycads, conifers and ferns grew widely. The first birds appeared. Marine reptiles and pterosaurs took many forms. Dinosaurs ruled the Earth!

203 mya

TRIASSIC PERIOD
Plants such as conifers, ginkgos, mosses and ferns were widespread. Reptiles and amphibians were common. The first dinosaurs, mammals, crocodiles and pterosaurs appeared.

250 mya

THE FIRST DINOSAURS

The time when dinosaurs lived on Earth is known as the Mesozoic Era. This is divided into three periods – the Triassic, Jurassic and Cretaceous. Dinosaurs first appeared in the Triassic Period.

DINO WORLD

The Earth was very different in the Triassic Period. There were no polar ice caps, no large inland seas and the climate was always dry and warm. These conditions were perfect for the dinosaurs to spread and to dominate the land. There were no flowering plants, but trees, such as conifers, cypresses and cycads flourished and ferns and mosses grew widely. These provided abundant food for plant-eating dinosaurs.

CHANGING PLANET

During the Triassic Period, the Earth's continents were all squashed together to form a huge supercontinent called Pangaea. This vast land mass lay right across the Equator, making temperatures very even. Animals and plants spread over Pangaea with ease as there were no great stretches of water to cross.

Over millions of years Pangaea broke up. By the close of the Jurassic Period, it had split into two new supercontinents – Laurasia and Gondwana. 150 million years later, at the end of the Cretaceous Period, these giant land masses had split into new, smaller continents. These are much the same as the ones we know today.

Plateosaurus had five-fingered hands with three claws. These could have been used to grasp branches when feeding, or to defend itself against predators.

TYRANNOSAURUS REX

(Tie-RAN-oh-SORE-us)

LIVED: 68–65 mya	**LENGTH:** 12.5m
PERIOD: Cretaceous	**HEIGHT:** 4m
LOCALITY: North America	**WEIGHT:** 6 tonnes
	DIET: carnivore

BUILT TO KILL

T.rex killed prey with crushing bites from its incredibly powerful jaws. Wounds found in fossil bones reveal how deeply it sank its teeth into its victims. Long, dagger-like teeth stabbed through flesh and its bite crunched through bone. *T. rex*'s arms were extremely small compared to its body size, so they were unlikely to have been used to hold struggling prey.

T. rex's teeth made deep and deadly puncture wounds.

Tyrannosaurus rex's teeth were up to 18cm long. The teeth of meat-eating dinosaurs continued to grow and be replaced throughout their lives. If a *T. rex* lost a tooth in a fight or an accident, a new one grew in its place.

AUGMENTED REALITY

Put your book on the floor or a table, then tap 💥 to open the crate and unleash a fearsome *Tyrannosaurus rex*. Use the joystick 🌱 to move *T. rex* around. Tap 🦕 to hear its mighty roar!

PREHISTORIC GIANTS

A palaeontologist works on the huge fossil neck vertebrae of a sauropod.

The largest creatures to have ever walked on land were planting-eating dinosaurs from the sauropod family. New fossil finds suggest that there may have been even bigger sauropods than those we already know about!

COLOSSAL CREATURES

Sauropods had four massive legs to support their incredible weight. These giant beasts had long necks, but very small heads compared to the size of their bodies. This design was well-suited for feeding on leaves, as a small head could fit easily amongst the treetop branches. Some sauropods had extremely long and flexible tails. The heaviest and tallest sauropod that we know about was probably *Amphicoelias*, which experts think weighed up to 100 tonnes.

Diplodocus' head was just 60cm long. The bones in its crane-like neck were partly hollow to make them lighter and more flexible.

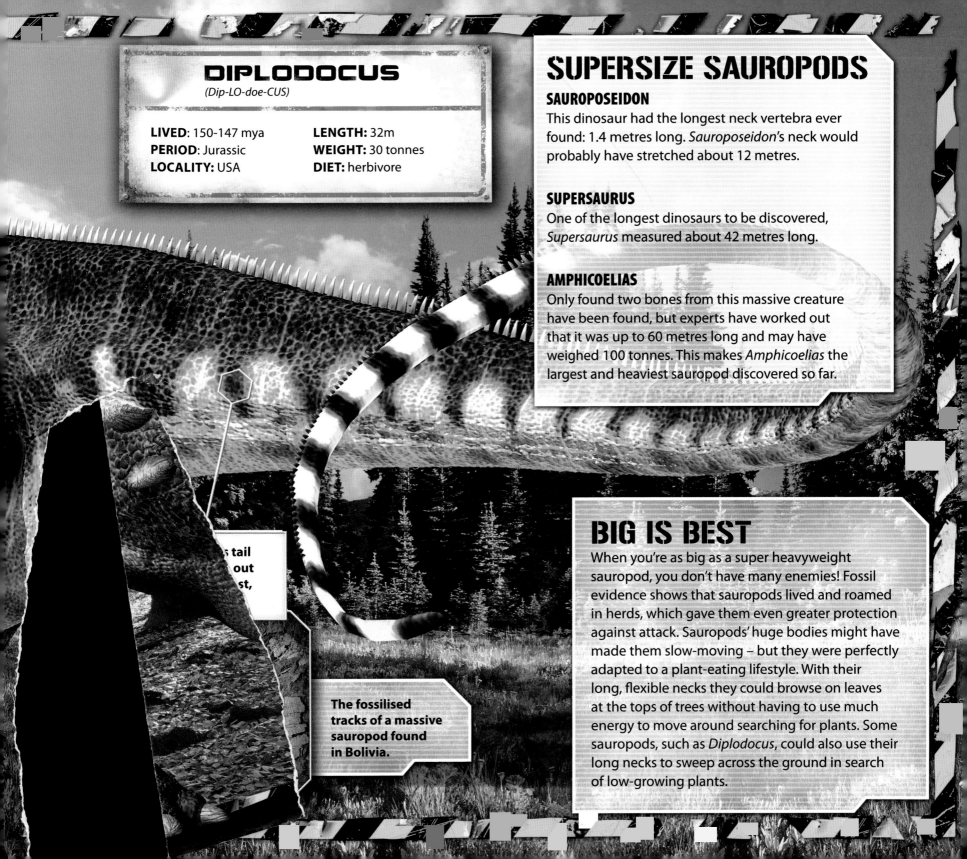

DIPLODOCUS
(Dip-LO-doe-CUS)

LIVED: 150-147 mya
PERIOD: Jurassic
LOCALITY: USA

LENGTH: 32m
WEIGHT: 30 tonnes
DIET: herbivore

SUPERSIZE SAUROPODS

SAUROPOSEIDON

This dinosaur had the longest neck vertebra ever found: 1.4 metres long. *Sauroposeidon*'s neck would probably have stretched about 12 metres.

SUPERSAURUS

One of the longest dinosaurs to be discovered, *Supersaurus* measured about 42 metres long.

AMPHICOELIAS

Only found two bones from this massive creature have been found, but experts have worked out that it was up to 60 metres long and may have weighed 100 tonnes. This makes *Amphicoelias* the largest and heaviest sauropod discovered so far.

... tail
... out
..., st,

The fossilised tracks of a massive sauropod found in Bolivia.

BIG IS BEST

When you're as big as a super heavyweight sauropod, you don't have many enemies! Fossil evidence shows that sauropods lived and roamed in herds, which gave them even greater protection against attack. Sauropods' huge bodies might have made them slow-moving – but they were perfectly adapted to a plant-eating lifestyle. With their long, flexible necks they could browse on leaves at the tops of trees without having to use much energy to move around searching for plants. Some sauropods, such as *Diplodocus*, could also use their long necks to sweep across the ground in search of low-growing plants.

ARMOURED ANKYLOSAURS

To defend themselves against predators, a group of dinosaurs called ankylosaurs developed tough armoured plates or spines. Some were also ready to fight back with spikes or club-like tails.

SUPER TOUGH

The ankylosaurs were among the best-protected dinosaurs. They had thick skin that was covered with tough bony plates and some had club-like tails that could deliver a deadly blow to predators.

These tank-like beasts were large and heavy, which made them difficult to push over. They also had short, powerful legs that let them spin around quickly to swing their tails at an enemy.

Only one fossil of an *Ankylosaurus* tail club has been found. It was long and flat, measuring about 60cm long and 30cm wide. Although relatively small it could still deliver a sledgehammer blow.

Edmontonia had sharp-edged spikes as well as bands of protective bony plates on its body.

ANKYLOSAURUS
(Ang-KIE-lo-SAWR-us)

LIVED: 70-65 mya
PERIOD: Late Cretaceous
LOCALITY: USA, Canada, South America
LENGTH: 7m

HEIGHT: 1.2m
WIDTH: 1.8m
WEIGHT: 6 tonnes
DIET: herbivore – ate low-lying plants, leaves and ferns

ARMOUR PLATED

Ankylosaurus was the largest of this group of armoured dinosaurs. It was also the most heavily armoured, with tough leathery skin on its upper body, studded with hard bony plates that acted like a suit of armour. These gave it protection from the teeth and claws of meat-eating predators, including *Tyrannosaurus rex*.

A blow to the legs from this hard tail club would disable a predator.

TAIL WEAPONS

A number of ankylosaurs had tails that could be used as a defensive weapon against attackers. *Euoplocephalus*, an elephant-sized ankylosaur, had a two-and-a-half-metre tail that ended in a club made from two bones joined together. Weighing up to 30 kg, this tail club could deliver terrible bone-crushing blows.

Ankylosaurus fed on low-lying plants and probably had a huge stomach to break down the vast amounts of tough plant material that it ate. This dinosaur would have produced huge amounts of gas!

STEGOSAURUS

Stegosaurus was the size of a bus and belongs to a group of dinosaurs called stegosaurs. All stegosaurs were plant-eaters, with strange bony plates along their backs and sharp spikes at the ends of their tails.

BIG AND SLOW

Stegosaurus was the biggest of the stegosaurs. The huge bony plates along its back would have made it look even bigger. It was a slow-moving herbivore, but its size and spiky tail would have put off predators, such as *Allosaurus*, which shared the same habitat.

THE PLATE DEBATE

Stegosaurus's bony plates were too thin to have been useful as armour. Some experts think that they were used to control body temperature, giving off heat to cool it down. It's also possible that they might have been brightly coloured and could have been used for display or to help identify other stegosaurs. They may even have changed colour to put off predators.

The smallest plates were on the neck, while the largest plates were over the hips and on the tail. These could be up to 70cm tall and 80cm wide.

STEGOSAURUS
(Steg-oh-sore-us)

LIVED: 155–145 mya
PERIOD: Late Jurassic
LOCALITY: USA, Portugal

LENGTH: 9m
DIET: herbivore – ate low-growing plants

DEADLY TAIL

Stegosaurus had four bony spikes that stuck out from the end of its tail. Each spike was around 90cm long. If attacked, *Stegosaurus* could swing its tail from side to side to deliver a blow with these large spikes. A lash from its tail would cause serious damage or even kill.

DUMB DINO?

Stegosaurus is famous for having the smallest brain of any known dinosaur. It was the size of a walnut, which is extremely small compared to its massive body. However, this does not mean that *Stegosaurus* was stupid. All plant-eating dinosaurs had a small brain relative to their huge size and this worked perfectly for the way they lived.

BIZARRE BEASTS

LIOPLEURODON
(LIE-oh-PLOO-ro-don)

LIVED: 165–145 mya
PERIOD: Jurassic
LOCALITY: UK, France and Germany
LENGTH: 15m

WEIGHT: 6 tonnes
DIET: carnivore – ate large sea creatures, such a squid or ichthyosaurs, plu fish and molluscs.

While dinosaurs dominated the land, sea reptiles, such as plesiosaurs, pliosaurs and ichthyosaurs, swam in the prehistoric oceans and flying reptiles called pterosaurs soared through the skies.

MONSTER OF THE DEEP

One of the greatest predators of the prehistoric seas and oceans was the pliosaur, *Liopleurodon*. This large marine reptile had flipper-shaped limbs, which it used to power itself through the murky Jurassic waters. It breathed air and, like all pliosaurs, it had a short and muscular neck compared to a plesiosaur.

Liopleurodon was huge. Its head and fearsome jaws were about 5 metres long. Like a modern-day shark, *Liopleurodon* had nostrils, so it might have tracked its prey by smell. It would have hunted and devoured giant turtles, plesiosaurs and ichthyosaurs.

Liopleurodon lived in deep waters and had few, if any predators, because of its huge size.

Ophthalmosaurus **was a predator, but it may have been the prey of deadly** *Liopleurodon*.

INCREDIBLE ICHTHYOSAURS

Ichthyosaurs were giant marine reptiles that looked like fish and dolphins. *Shastasaurus* is the largest ichthyosaur to have been discovered. At 21 metres in length, it was the largest prehistoric sea reptile. Another ichthyosaur, *Ophthalmosaurus*, had huge eyes, up to 23cm wide, which helped it to spot prey in the deep, dark waters of the ocean.

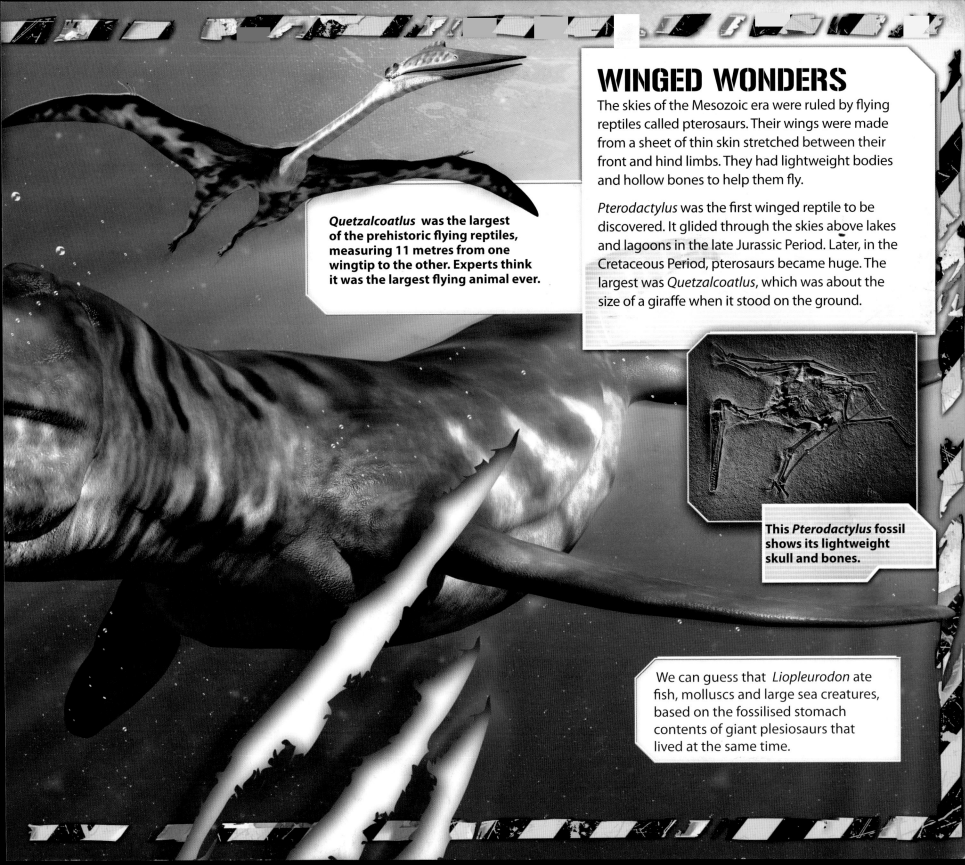

Quetzalcoatlus was the largest of the prehistoric flying reptiles, measuring 11 metres from one wingtip to the other. Experts think it was the largest flying animal ever.

WINGED WONDERS

The skies of the Mesozoic era were ruled by flying reptiles called pterosaurs. Their wings were made from a sheet of thin skin stretched between their front and hind limbs. They had lightweight bodies and hollow bones to help them fly.

Pterodactylus was the first winged reptile to be discovered. It glided through the skies above lakes and lagoons in the late Jurassic Period. Later, in the Cretaceous Period, pterosaurs became huge. The largest was *Quetzalcoatlus*, which was about the size of a giraffe when it stood on the ground.

This *Pterodactylus* fossil shows its lightweight skull and bones.

We can guess that *Liopleurodon* ate fish, molluscs and large sea creatures, based on the fossilised stomach contents of giant plesiosaurs that lived at the same time.

BRACHIOSAURUS

Brachiosaurus was a plant-eating dinosaur from the sauropod family. Although it wasn't the tallest of the giant sauropods, its long front legs meant that *Brachiosaurus* could reach the highest in order to feed.

Brachiosaurus had large nostrils, so dinosaur experts believe it would have had a powerful sense of smell.

A BIG EATER

Brachiosaurus weighed around 35 tonnes, about the same as seven elephants, which are the largest land-based animals on Earth today. Being so enormous meant that *Brachiosaurus* would have had to spend most of its time eating to maintain its massive body weight. Grazing in herds, this giant dinosaur would have fed on plants such as conifers, cycads, ferns and ginkgo trees. It may have eaten about 400kg of leafy plant material every day.

When it first hatched from its egg, a *Brachiosaurus* baby would probably have been about the size of a human baby.

EATING HABITS

Brachiosaurus had short jaw bones, with 52 small, sharp, chisel-shaped teeth, perfectly adapted for nipping and cropping leaves. It didn't chew its dinner, it just swallowed it whole. To digest the tough vegetation that it ate, *Brachiosaurus* had a huge gut, which slowly broke down the plant matter over a period of a few days.

The only complete *Brachiosaurus* skull was discovered in 1998. Like other sauropods, *Brachiosaurus* had a small head on a huge body.

REACHING THE TOP

Brachiosaurus was the only sauropod to have front legs that were longer than its back legs. Scientists believe that these longer front legs allowed the *Brachiosaurus* to raise its long neck and tiny head up to graze on the leaves at the very tops of the trees. *Brachiosaurus* could stretch up to eat, but it would not have been able to rear up onto its two back legs as they would have been unable to support its massive body weight.

DINOSAUR EGGS

Dinosaur babies hatched from eggs and, although relatively rare, fossilised eggs have been found at more than 200 sites across the world. The eggs of sauropods like *Brachiosaurus* were football-shaped and had a thick protective shell.

EGG LAYING

Some sauropods appear to have laid their eggs in rows, while others have been laid in clusters. It is thought that giant sauropods like *Brachiosaurus* must have laid their eggs using a long tube that extended from their bodies. The eggs may have been covered over with sand or soil to protect them from hungry predators.

DINOSAUR BABIES

Fossil finds, including eggs and dinosaur babies, show that while some dinosaurs cared for their eggs and young, others left their hatchlings to fend for themselves. *Brachiosaurus* babies, like other sauropod hatchlings, probably had to guard against predators as soon as they emerged from their shells.

A *Brachiosaurus* egg would have been roughly spherical and about 30cm long by 25cm wide.

AUGMENTED REALITY

Tap 💥 to hatch a baby *Brachiosaurus* from its egg, then help it to take its first steps by moving it about with the joystick control 🕹. Tap 🦕 to hear your baby dinosaur call out!

HORNS AND HEADGEAR

Several groups of plant-eating dinosaurs had impressive headgear, such as horns, frills, crests, or tough bony domes. These were used for protection, self-defence or display.

TRIPLE-HORNED TERROR

Triceraptops was one of the largest and most common of the horned dinosaurs. It was as long as a bus and had a huge skull over 2 metres long – nearly a third of its total body length! Its head sported two long brow horns and a shorter snout horn. These deadly weapons protected it from predators such as *Tyrannosaurus rex*, or other rival *Triceratops*. Over 50 *Triceratops* skulls have been found and some of these fossil remains have *Tyrannosaurus* teeth marks in them, or show scars from wounds made by *Triceratops* horns.

Triceratops's bony frill could be up to 1m wide. Experts believe that it was used for display and attracting mates.

HEADSTRONG DINOS

CERATOPSIANS
These bulky beasts all had backward-facing bony frills, as well as horns and hooked, beak-like mouths.

HADROSAURS
Also known as duck-billed dinosaurs, they had colourful bony crests and long flattened beaks.

PACHYCEPHALOSAURS
These had hard skulls with bony bumps, which could have been used like a battering ram.

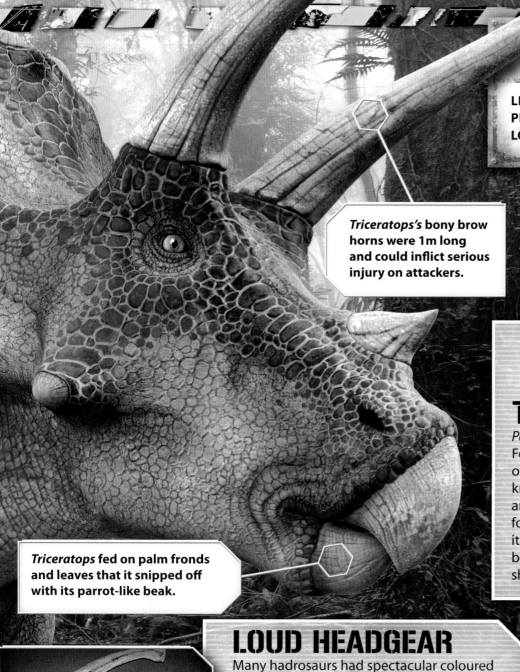

TRICERATOPS
(Try-SER-ah-tops)

LIVED: 67–65 mya
PERIOD: Late Cretaceous
LOCALITY: USA, Canada

LENGTH: 9m
WEIGHT: 5.5 tonnes
DIET: herbivore

Triceratops's bony brow horns were 1m long and could inflict serious injury on attackers.

Pachycephalosaurus's skull had a large dome of hard bone.

THICK SKULLED

Pachycephalosaurus's name means "thick-headed lizard". Fossils of its massive skull reveal that it had a dome-shape bulge on top of the head that was covered in tough bony bumps and knobs. The dome was made of solid bone about 25cm thick and this suggests that *Pachycephalosaurus* used its thick head for butting. Some experts think that *Pachycephalosaurus* used its bony head in battles with rival males and that the joint between its skull and neck was designed to absorb the shock from using its head as a battering ram.

Triceratops fed on palm fronds and leaves that it snipped off with its parrot-like beak.

LOUD HEADGEAR

Many hadrosaurs had spectacular coloured head crests, but *Parasaurolophus* had the strangest crest of them all. It was about 2 metres long and was hollow, with looped air passages inside. It is thought that *Parasaurolophus* blew through this crest to make sounds to attract mates or as a warning to scare off rivals and predators.

Two rival male Triceratops prepare to lock horns.

VICIOUS VELOCIRAPTOR

Velociraptor was a small predator that lived in the hot, dry deserts of Asia in the late Cretaceous Period. It was a deadly hunter with a large, curved claw on each foot that could deal out vicious wounds to prey.

FEATHERED PREDATOR

The first *Velociraptor* fossils were discovered in Mongolia's Gobi Desert in 1922. Since then, a dozen or so other fossil skeletons and remains have been found in Russia, China and Mongolia. These fossils show that *Velociraptor* was about the size of an adult turkey and walked on two legs. Small quill-knobs on the forelimbs show that it had feathers, but they weren't used for flight. It's more likely that the feathers were used to control body temperature and for display.

Velociraptor's long jaw was packed with about 60 small, sharp teeth for tearing at flesh.

SMART HUNTERS

Velociraptors had relatively large brains for their body size, making them intelligent hunters, with keen senses of sight and smell and quick reflexes. These features allowed them to be agile, successful predators. Their short legs meant that they probably wouldn't have been very speedy over a long distance, but they could probably have run at speeds of up to 39km/h for short bursts of time when hunting.

THE RAPTOR FAMILY

Palaeontologists use the term "dromaeosaurid" (*dro-may-o-saw-id*) to describe *Velociraptor* and other raptor-type dinosaurs. The name means "running lizard" and describes a group of bipedal (standing on two feet) carnivorous dinosaurs. This group of bird-like dinosaurs were agile hunters, with sharp teeth, large eyes and a sickle-shaped toe claw. Other raptors include *Deinonychus* and *Utahraptor*.

An enlarged 9cm claw on the second toe of each foot could have delivered deadly stabbing wounds to prey.

VELOCIRAPTOR

(Vel-O-si-RAP-tor)

LIVED: 75 to 71 mya
PERIOD: Late Cretaceous
LOCALITY: Mongolia, China and Russia
LENGTH: up to 2.5m
HEIGHT: up to 1m
WEIGHT: 7kg to15kg
DIET: carnivore – ate small mammals and dinosaurs

DUELLING DINOSAURS

In 1971, palaeontologists discovered the complete skeletal remains of a *Velociraptor* and a *Protoceratops* who had died while locked in combat. This amazing fossil revealed a lot about the fighting, killing and feeding habits of *Velociraptor*. This small, agile, predator preyed on small dinosaurs like the pig-sized *Protoceratops*. It used its three-fingered claws to grasp and hold down its prey, while it slashed, jabbed and stabbed at its victim with the long, sickle-shaped claws on its feet. It could also have given its victim nasty bites with its razor-sharp teeth. However, the fossil also shows that *Protoceratops* put up a good fight. It had one of the *Velociraptor*'s arms clamped in its beaked jaws when they died.

A long, stiff tail acted as a counterbalance when *Velociraptor* was running or kicking out with its sickle-clawed feet.

AUGMENTED REALITY

Tap 📦 to open the crate and go hunting with a pack of *Velociraptors*. Steer your *Velociraptor* around with the joystick 🐾 and watch the rest follow. Tap 🦶 to hear your dino roar!

DINOSAUR DINNERS

Giganotosaurus's huge jaws were packed with 20cm-long saw-edged teeth.

What did dinosaurs eat? Like other animals, some dinosaurs ate plants, some ate meat (hunted or scavenged) and some ate both. Their bodies, teeth and jaws, were adapted to suit their particular diets.

GIGANTIC GUTS

Huge plant-eating sauropods, such as *Brachiosaurus*, needed to eat about a tonne of vegetation everyday. Their peg-like teeth were designed to rake in the vegetation from trees, but were no good for chewing. In order to break down massive meals of tough plant material, sauropods needed enormous guts. They would also have produced a lot of gas!

VEGGIE-SAURS

Smaller herbivores, such as the hadrosaurs (duck-billed dinosaurs) and ceratopsians (horned dinosaurs), had teeth that were designed to break down leafy food. The hadrosaur *Edmontosaurus* used its duck-like beak to browse on plants, which it then ground down with over 1,000 cheek teeth. Ceratopsians, such as *Triceratops* and *Protoceratops*, used their sharp-edged beaks to slice and tear leaves from plants and trees. At the back of their jaws they had special self-sharpening teeth to chop and slice up their food.

Giganotosaurus may have used its massive body weight to slam into its victims, knocking them over before sinking its teeth into them.

The fossil skull of a *Protoceratops* shows its sharp beak for slicing leaves and shoots.

GIGANOTOSAURUS

(Jig-a-NOT-o-SAW-rus)

LIVED: 100 mya
PERIOD: Cretaceous
LOCALITY: South America
LENGTH: 12.5m

HEIGHT: up to 4m
WEIGHT: 8 tonnes
DIET: carnivore – ate meat, including even very large dinosaurs

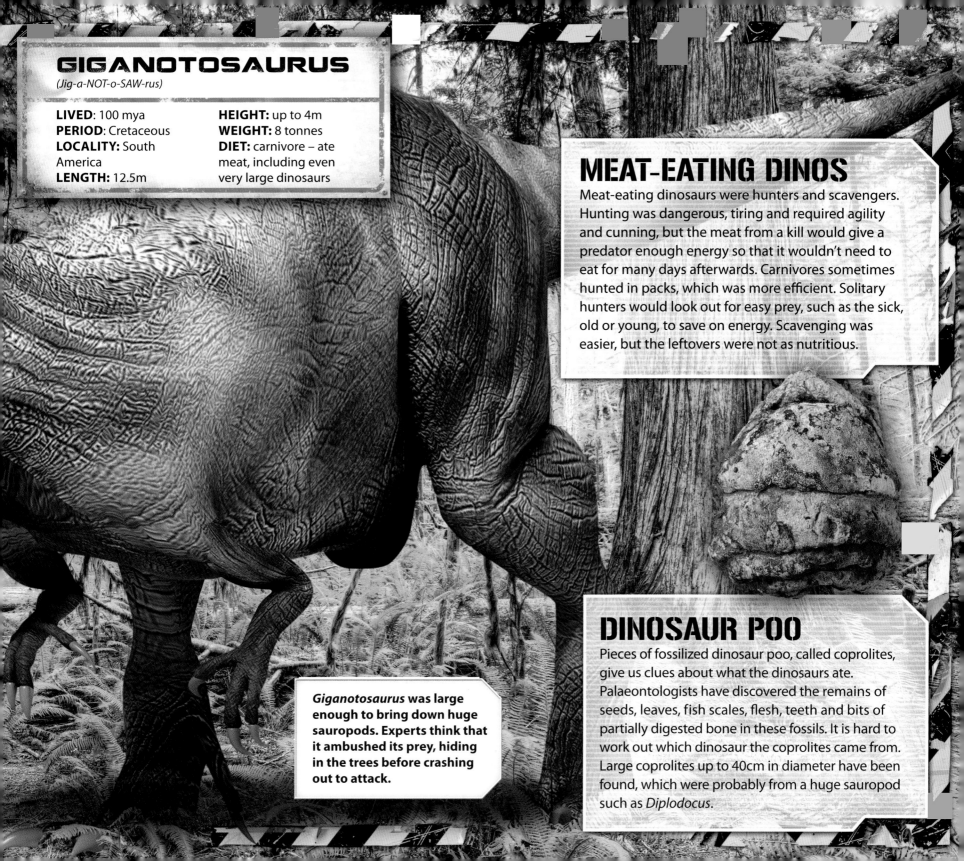

MEAT-EATING DINOS

Meat-eating dinosaurs were hunters and scavengers. Hunting was dangerous, tiring and required agility and cunning, but the meat from a kill would give a predator enough energy so that it wouldn't need to eat for many days afterwards. Carnivores sometimes hunted in packs, which was more efficient. Solitary hunters would look out for easy prey, such as the sick, old or young, to save on energy. Scavenging was easier, but the leftovers were not as nutritious.

Giganotosaurus **was large enough to bring down huge sauropods. Experts think that it ambushed its prey, hiding in the trees before crashing out to attack.**

DINOSAUR POO

Pieces of fossilized dinosaur poo, called coprolites, give us clues about what the dinosaurs ate. Palaeontologists have discovered the remains of seeds, leaves, fish scales, flesh, teeth and bits of partially digested bone in these fossils. It is hard to work out which dinosaur the coprolites came from. Large coprolites up to 40cm in diameter have been found, which were probably from a huge sauropod such as *Diplodocus*.

HIGH-FLYING PTERANODON

Pterosaurs were flying reptiles that lived at the same time as the dinosaurs. *Pteranodon* was one of the largest of the pterosaurs and ruled the prehistoric skies of the Late Cretaceous Period.

WINGED GIANT

Pteranodon had huge wings, much larger than any known bird. An adult male's wings could stretch up to 10 metres wide. The wings weren't feathered, but were made of a leathery, skin-like membrane, which stretched between the body, the top of each leg and an elongated fourth finger on each hand. Like a bird, *Pteranodon* had lightweight, hollow bones, which made it easier to lift its huge body into the air.

Pteranodon's long beak-like jaw had no teeth.

Experts think that *Pteranodon* folded up its wings to walk upright on all fours over short distances.

AUGMENTED REALITY

Tap (🎆) to open the crate and to send a mighty *Pteranodon* soaring through the air. Steer it about with the joystick. Tap (✈) to hear its call. Tap on (⬍) to make it land, (⬍) to make it fly again or (↻) to put it back into the crate!

CLEARED FOR TAKEOFF!

Pteranodon probably took off from the ground rather than launching itself from high places like cliffs. With a quick burst of energy it used its long forelimbs to 'pole vault' into the air. As soon as it had cleared the ground, it flapped its massive wings to gain height.

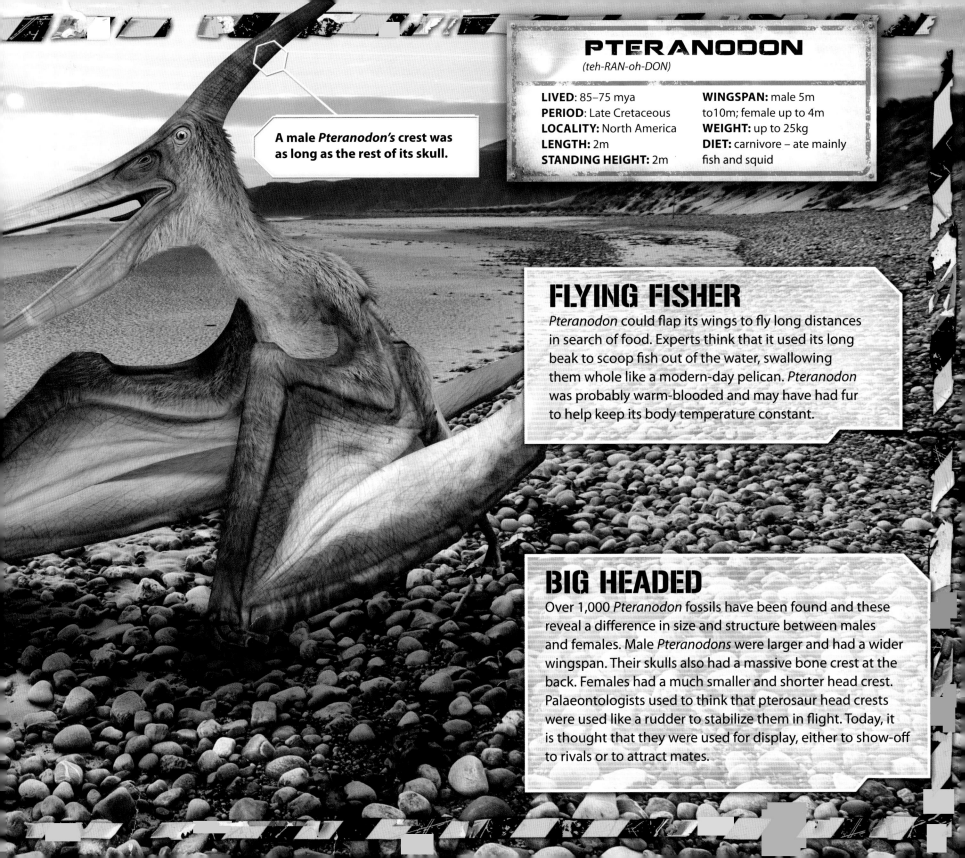

PTERANODON
(teh-RAN-oh-DON)

LIVED: 85–75 mya
PERIOD: Late Cretaceous
LOCALITY: North America
LENGTH: 2m
STANDING HEIGHT: 2m

WINGSPAN: male 5m to10m; female up to 4m
WEIGHT: up to 25kg
DIET: carnivore – ate mainly fish and squid

A male *Pteranodon's* crest was as long as the rest of its skull.

FLYING FISHER
Pteranodon could flap its wings to fly long distances in search of food. Experts think that it used its long beak to scoop fish out of the water, swallowing them whole like a modern-day pelican. *Pteranodon* was probably warm-blooded and may have had fur to help keep its body temperature constant.

BIG HEADED
Over 1,000 *Pteranodon* fossils have been found and these reveal a difference in size and structure between males and females. Male *Pteranodons* were larger and had a wider wingspan. Their skulls also had a massive bone crest at the back. Females had a much smaller and shorter head crest. Palaeontologists used to think that pterosaur head crests were used like a rudder to stabilize them in flight. Today, it is thought that they were used for display, either to show-off to rivals or to attract mates.

END OF THE DINOSAURS

About 65 million years ago, the dinosaurs suddenly disappeared, along with more than half of all the animal life on Earth. Scientists have various theories to explain this mass extinction.

METEORITE IMPACT

There is evidence that a huge meteorite may have struck the Earth at the end of the Cretaceous Period, wiping out plant life, the dinosaurs and other creatures. In 1990, a vast meteorite crater, 180km across, and dating from about 65 million years ago, was found on the seabed off Mexico. The size of the crater suggests a meteorite 10km wide may have hit the Earth at 100,000km/h.

CHAIN REACTION

An immense meteorite impact would have triggered a series of volcanic eruptions and tsunamis that would have devastated low-lying coastal areas. The gases, dust and ash thrown into the atmosphere would have caused extreme climate changes, killing most plants and the animals that depended on them for food.

SUDDEN DEATH

Fossil finds show that there was a relatively sudden extinction of dinosaurs, pterosaurs and giant sea reptiles around 65 million years ago. Rather than a gradual decline due to changes in climate, this suggests a catastrophic event on a global scale. The two most widely accepted theories are that a large meteorite struck the Earth, or that there were widespread volcanic eruptions. These could have caused devastating environmental damage, leading to the extinction of a vast amount of animal life.

A skull belonging to _Edmontosaurus_, one of the last surviving dinosaurs.